GIANTS of RAP and HIP-HOP

DRAKE

Bradley Steffens

ReferencePoint Press®

San Diego, CA

About the Author

Bradley Steffens is a poet, a novelist, and an award-winning author of more than fifty nonfiction books for children and young adults.

For more information, contact:
ReferencePoint Press, Inc.
PO Box 27779
San Diego, CA 92198
www.ReferencePointPress.com

LIBRARY OF CONGRESS CATALOGING-IN-PUBLICATION DATA

Names: Steffens, Bradley, 1955– author.
Title: Drake/by Bradley Steffens.
Description: San Diego: ReferencePoint Press, 2020. | Series: Giants of
  Rap and Hip-Hop | Includes bibliographical references and index. |
  Audience: Grades 10–12
Identifiers: LCCN 2019027031 (print) | LCCN 2019027032 (ebook) | ISBN
  9781682827710 (library binding) | ISBN 9781682827727 (ebook)
Subjects: LCSH: Drake, 1986—Juvenile literature. | Rap
  musicians—Canada—Juvenile literature.
Classification: LCC ML3930.D73 S74 2020 (print) | LCC ML3930.D73 (ebook)
  | DDC 782.421649092 [B]—dc23
LC record available at https://lccn.loc.gov/2019027031
LC ebook record available at https://lccn.loc.gov/2019027032

Contents

Introduction   4
Record Setter

Chapter One   8
The Family Business

Chapter Two   17
Television Star

Chapter Three   26
Self-Produced Stardom

Chapter Four   36
Chart Topper

Chapter Five   46
Branching Out

Source Notes   55
Important Events in the Life of Drake   58
For More Information   60
Index   61
Picture Credits   64

CONTENTS

RECORD SETTER

In July 2018 Aubrey Drake Graham, known by his stage name Drake, broke a record set more than fifty years earlier by the best-selling recording artists of all time, The Beatles. It was a record many thought would never be equaled, let alone broken. During that week, Drake had seven of the top ten songs on the *Billboard* Hot 100 chart, two more than The Beatles had in April 1964. It would have been an amazing feat for anyone to accomplish, but what made it even more jaw-dropping is the fact that Drake is a rap and hip-hop artist, performing in a genre that rarely tops the Hot 100 chart.

Drake's dominance of the *Billboard* Top 100 did not come as a total surprise to industry insiders. After all, he had already broken many *Billboard* chart records. In less than a decade, he had surpassed Lil Wayne as the solo artist with the most charted songs in the history of the *Billboard* Hot 100—a total of 203. He has also had more number one singles on *Billboard*'s Hot Rap Songs than any rapper to date and more number one songs on the Hot R&B/Hip-Hop Airplay and Rhythmic charts than anyone else. All five of his studio albums have reached number one on the *Billboard* album charts and have been certified as platinum by the Recording Industry Association of America (RIAA), with sales of more than 1 million units each. The RIAA has also certified that Drake has sold more digital singles than any artist in history. In 2018 he became the first artist to surpass 50 billion audio streams, or online plays of his songs, across all global streaming platforms.

A Multitalented Artist

Drake is more than a record-setting performer. He is also the composer and lyricist of his songs. While this is not unusual in the rap world, it does set him apart from many of the best-selling singers of all time. That group includes Elvis Presley, Frank Sinatra, and Whitney Houston—all of whom rarely wrote their own songs. As a creative force, Drake is more in the mold of rappers like Lil Wayne, Kanye West, and Jay-Z and songwriters like Prince and Michael Jackson. Most significantly, Drake has broken new ground by combining rapping with singing in a seamless style that has become his signature sound.

Part of Drake's appeal is visual—an important factor in the music video era. He is a handsome man who is a trained actor, having spent several years as a cast member of the popular Canadian television program *Degrassi: The Next Generation*. Not only is he at home in front of the camera, but his acting abilities make the nonmusical vignettes in his music videos convincing and effective. He has returned to his acting roots on more than one occasion, most notably as the voice of the wooly mammoth Ethan in the 2012 animated movie *Ice Age: Continental Drift*.

Drake's acting skills have made him a successful spokesperson for commercial brands like Sprite, Apple Music, and the world champion Toronto Raptors of the National Basketball Association (NBA). He is also an entrepreneur, developing a clothing line, athletic shoes, and even a bourbon whiskey. In June 2019 *Forbes* estimated Drake's net worth at $150 million.

A Search for Love

Despite his vast wealth and global fame—or perhaps because of it—Drake has yet to find a partner in life, a fact he laments in song after song. Drake's parents split up when he was five, and he was raised by his mother, who showered him with affection, attention, and love. So far, he says, no one else has shown him the pure, unconditional love he received at home. Since becoming a superstar, he has found that many women are attracted to him, but most seem more interested in his fame, his money, or what he can do for their careers than in having a serious relationship with him. At the same time, the memory of his parents' breakup makes

Rapper and hip-hop artist Drake wows a New Orleans crowd in 2018. That same year, Drake had seven of the top ten songs on the Billboard Hot 100 chart—breaking a record set by The Beatles in 1964.

Drake reluctant to become too deeply involved with anyone. He discusses these struggles in his music in a way that few artists, and even fewer rappers, have before, making his quest for love an epic saga of his time. He says he has no choice but to do so. "I'm a very honest person," he says. "I can't write fiction. I can't really do these sort of like themed story songs about someone else I made up. It all has to directly do with me or I can't make the music."[1]

For now, everything Drake touches turns to gold. However, the music business is a fast-changing world, and few stars have remained at the top for very long. Drake's talents as a songwriter and an actor in addition to being a singer will certainly help his longevity. It may be that his era has just begun.

> "I can't write fiction. I can't really do these sort of like themed story songs about someone else I made up. It all has to directly do with me or I can't make the music."[1]
>
> —Drake

CHAPTER ONE

THE FAMILY BUSINESS

Aubrey Drake Graham was born on October 24, 1986, in Toronto, Canada. At the time of Drake's birth, his mother, Sandi Graham, was a twenty-six-year-old schoolteacher from Toronto. His father, Dennis Graham, was a professional drummer from Memphis, Tennessee. The professions of Drake's parents—one emphasizing language skills and the other emphasizing music—would play a big part in shaping his interests. "My mom used to force me to say things as colorfully as possible," Drake remembers. "She would never let me get by with saying 'Well that food was good.' No, I had to say, 'That food was delicious,' or something extravagant. My mom was responsible for a lot of the way I write, the way I choose to say things. That's where the music comes in on my mom's side."[2]

Raised with Faith

Drake's mother is white and Jewish; his father is African American and Catholic. His parents split up when he was five years old. His father returned to Memphis, and his mother remained in Toronto with her son. The separation was difficult for Drake, who only got to see his father during the summer.

Sandi raised her son in the Jewish faith. "I identify as Jewish," says Drake. "I am a person who, you know, I talk to God. I just try to live a very good life, to be a good person. I'm not necessarily extremely religious, but my mom and I always do the high holidays together."[3]

When he was thirteen, Drake formally celebrated his elevation to adulthood in Judaism with a bar mitzvah ceremony. Twelve years later, in 2011, he reaffirmed his faith by having a second bar mitzvah. "When I had a Bar Mitzvah back in the day, my mom really didn't have that much money," Drake explains. "We kinda just did it in the basement of an Italian restaurant, which I guess is kinda like a faux pas. I told myself that if I ever got rich, I'd throw myself a re-Bar Mitzvah."[4]

A Family of Musicians

Drake's father played drums for rockabilly star Jerry Lee Lewis for many years, but he is not the only professional musician in the family. Drake's uncles, his father's brothers, were even bigger musical successes. One uncle is Larry Graham, the bassist for Sly and the Family Stone, a groundbreaking group that fused funk, soul, and rock music. Another uncle, Mabon Lewis "Teenie" Hodges, was the lead guitarist with renowned rhythm and blues (R&B) singer Al Green. The success of these family members made show business seem more like a normal, everyday job than a far-off dream.

Drake's father loved classic R&B music and played it all the time, especially in the car on the long drives from Toronto to Memphis and back when Drake would visit Memphis during summer vacation. "I used to drive down here all the time in this Mercury Cougar . . . and that's where I got a lot of music knowledge, actually," Drake told a meeting of the National Academy of Recording Arts and Sciences in Nashville, Tennessee, in 2009. "My dad used to give me 30 minutes to play hip hop on the 24 or 25 hour drive—he'd let me put on rap tapes and then he'd make me listen to Marvin Gaye, The Spinners . . . that really penetrated my mind as a young kid."[5] The influence of the music his father played would later show up in many of Drake's recordings, as he incorporated singing into his rap songs and then began to sing entire tracks in the R&B style.

> "My dad used to . . . make me listen to Marvin Gaye, The Spinners . . . that really penetrated my mind as a young kid."[5]
>
> —Drake

Drake and his mother, Sandi Graham, pose for a photo at the 2011 Canadian Academy of Recording Arts and Sciences Juno Awards. Drake credits his mother's influence for how he writes and expresses himself in his music.

Drake's father also introduced his son to performing at a young age. When Drake was about nine years old, his father took him along on one of his gigs. At one point during the performance, he brought Drake onstage and had him sing the only song he knew, the R&B classic "Mustang Sally." Drake says, "I ended up onstage performing with my dad, and everyone thought it was the cutest thing in the world. I don't remember much about my childhood, but I remember that night."[6]

A Talent for Language

Sandi Graham also noticed that her son had special gifts, including a flair for rhyming. "We always thought there was something very different about this kid," she recalls. "When we had a piano at home and I would come home with my nursery rhymes, Aubrey at three years old would take the lyrics and he would change them. I realized that other kids just didn't do that."[7]

"I would come home with my nursery rhymes, Aubrey at three years old would take the lyrics and he would change them. I realized that other kids just didn't do that."[7]

—Sandi Graham, Drake's mother

Sandi also noticed that her son had the exotic, mixed-race good looks that were coming into fashion in the advertising industry. When he was five years old, she took him to a modeling agent, who accepted him as a client. The agent found the boy work in print ads, catalogs, and television commercials.

Building on Drake's modeling success, Sandi enrolled her son in the Toronto Young People's Theatre. Although Drake would later dismiss this experience as just a bunch of young kids who would throw on masks and call it a play, he learned important fundamentals about acting, including memorizing lines, speaking on cue, and following a director's instructions about where to move and stand on the stage. These acting basics would serve him well when he ventured into the television industry.

The Young People's Theatre also showed him the power of a good performance and the bond it can create with the audience. After a performance of the period musical *Les Misérables*, the audience gave the young performers a long, enthusiastic ovation. "*Les Mis* was the first thing that people actually liked, I guess, and people actually came to see, and clapped for a good reason, not like, 'Yay, it's over,' like, 'Good, let's go home,'"[8] Drake says.

An Outsider

Despite Drake's successful forays into the entertainment world and the love and encouragement he received at home, his childhood

A Harry Potter Fan

Like millions of other kids around the world, Drake grew up reading the Harry Potter series of books by J.K. Rowling. As an adult, Drake showed his appreciation for the series by posting a picture on Instagram from one of the Harry Potter movies. The digitally altered photo shows three boys seated in the Great Hall of Hogwarts with Drake's face in place of Draco Malfoy's. The picture was accompanied by the hashtag #DrakeOMalfoy.

In a 2017 interview with Tatiana Siegel of the *Hollywood Reporter*, Drake said that he was interested in buying a signed, first edition of *Harry Potter and the Sorcerer's Stone*, the first book in Rowling's series. Only five hundred hardback copies of the first edition were printed, making the book extremely rare. The copy that came onto the market in 2017 was priced at $160,000. "I should get it," Drake told Siegel. "My birthday's coming up. Maybe I'll buy it for myself as a treat." In June 2018 the entertainment website Zimbio reported that Drake had indeed purchased the book.

Quoted in Tatiana Siegel, "Drake's Hotline to Hollywood: Inside an Ambitious Push into Film and TV," *Hollywood Reporter*, November 8, 2017. www.hollywoodreporter.com.

was not ideal. The separation of his parents brought sadness and loss into his young life. He longed to connect with other kids, but he discovered that it was not easy. Rejection by girls was especially painful. "I used to cry a lot in school," he recalls. "I used to fall for girls so hard. And be so reluctant to embrace those emotions."[9]

Drake also experienced racial bias at a young age. Attending school in the predominantly white, Jewish area of Toronto known as Forest Hill, Drake was sometimes teased for being mixed race. "I was actually the closest thing to a black person at my school, and it was a very painful process and time. Kids don't always understand," he recalls. "It wasn't necessarily that I was black that bothered them, it was that they didn't understand me being black and Jewish."[10] He told *Heeb* magazine that his classmates called him *schwartze*, the Yiddish word for "black"—a word that is often also used in a derogatory way.

One particularly painful moment came when Drake attended the birthday party of a classmate. He was excited to go because he was not invited to many parties, and he knew that a girl he liked was going to be there. When he arrived, however, he learned that the kids had a secret motive for inviting him. He recalls:

> I showed up and there was this picture of me on the door in a Power Rangers costume, from like a Wal-Mart photo ad. And I realized they invited me so they could make fun of me. But I was too embarrassed to call my mom to pick me up, so I actually walked an hour and a half home from this party, because I didn't want her to think I didn't have a good time. Suffice to say I really did not like going to that school, and I wanted to go somewhere where there was more variety.[11]

Things were not much better when Drake visited his father's family in Memphis, Tennessee. There, he felt like an outcast because he was half white and had what other kids considered a privileged background. "I remember for a lot of my life, being ashamed of who I was, or not confident in who I was, sort of, just different things, like the fact that I was more emotional than other kids,"[12] he recalls. He poured out his feelings in words, writing poetry and rap lyrics for himself. "I've been writing since I was really young," he says. "I wrote about how I viewed the world, like not having my dad around or being biracial."[13]

"I was actually the closest thing to a black person at my school, and it was a very painful process and time."[10]

—Drake

Harsh Realities

Although teased by the black side of his family for living in a wealthy neighborhood, Drake was no stranger to the African American experience. He learned firsthand how African Americans are treated by the police on one of the summer vacation road trips coming back from Memphis. His father was stopped at the US-Canada border because he was facing criminal charges and not allowed to leave the country. "I saw my dad get arrested by like a SWAT team at the border for trying to cross over," Drake recalls. "I've seen things that didn't make me happy. They were character building. That's why I think people in the 'hood can still connect with what I'm saying."[14]

Drake learned more about the hard side of life when his father spent two years in jail in Memphis. Although Drake did not visit his father in person, he did speak with him by phone. He heard directly from his father about the harsh conditions and the loneliness of the inmates.

The hardship of prison life became even clearer when Drake spoke with his father's cell mate, a man in his early twenties who did not have many visitors or anyone outside of prison to talk

Drake says his taste in music was influenced by his musician father, Dennis Graham. On long drives with his father, the pair often listened to Marvin Gaye (pictured) and other R&B artists.

Drake Thanks His Mom

At the 2019 *Billboard* Music Awards, held at the MGM Grand Garden Arena in Las Vegas and broadcast live on NBC, Drake received twelve awards, including the award for Top Artist. In his Top Artist acceptance speech, Drake dedicated the award to his mother and publicly thanked her for the upbringing she gave him:

> I just want to thank my mom for her relentless effort in my life. I want to thank my mom for all the times you drove me to piano when I didn't want to take piano. All the times you drove me to basketball and hockey—that clearly didn't work out. All the times you drove me to *Degrassi*. No matter how long it took me to figure out what I wanted to do, you were always there to give me a ride, and now we're on one hell of ride. So, thank you, I appreciate it.

Quoted in Nicholas Hautman, "Drake Breaks Taylor Swift's Record for Most *Billboard* Music Award Wins," *Us Weekly*, May 2, 2019. www.usmagazine.com.

to. Although Drake was a virtual stranger, the young prisoner reached out to him. He told Drake that he loved rap music and went by the rap name Poverty. He performed his raps on the phone to Drake. When Drake mentioned that he also wrote rap lyrics, Poverty asked to hear them. Drake practiced his raps at home and then performed them on the phone when he called his father. The experience had a profound effect on Drake, who had turned to writing as an outlet for his sadness and pain but had kept his work to himself. "That was actually the first person where I technically rapped," he recalls. "It was a cool little thing that allowed me to realize that I can rap the things that I write down."[15]

Rapping with Poverty became a turning point in Drake's life. He realized that rap music was not just something to listen to but was also an outlet for his deepest emotions. He began to study hip-hop music, observing the different beats, flows, and rhyme

Pharrell Williams (shown performing in the Netherlands in 2018) was an early influence on Drake's music. Some of Drake's first experiences with rap music included studying the beats, flows, and rhyme schemes of rappers such as Williams.

schemes of professional rappers like Pharrell Williams, Nas, and the Notorious B.I.G. He began to see how technique could be used to strengthen his message. "I remember being seventeen and I really started to fall in love with the whole Star Trak movement," he told MTV, referring to the record label started by Pharrell Williams and his fellow producer Chad Hugo. "I'll never forget Pharrell and the Neptunes. Pharrell and his whole movement really made me care about music."[16] Although Drake enjoyed modeling and acting, music was becoming the center of his life.

TELEVISION STAR

At age thirteen Drake had a strong interest in the arts. He had both sung and acted onstage in front of live audiences. He had modeled professionally and been in television commercials. He enjoyed writing rhyming verse in his private notebooks. It was unclear which, if any, of these interests he would pursue seriously. That changed in 1999, when a classmate introduced Drake to his father, a talent agent.

A Big Break

The classmate's father was in search of a teen actor to audition for the television series *Degrassi: The Next Generation*, a Canadian teen drama television series set at the fictional Degrassi Community School. The classmate's father had asked his son if there was anyone at school who could make the other kids laugh. The boy immediately thought of Drake, and his father asked to meet him. The agent was impressed with Drake's looks, personality, and speaking voice. He arranged for Drake to audition for *Degrassi*, a program that was known for its ensemble casts and willingness to dramatize hard-hitting subjects, including bullying, drug abuse, mental disorders, gang violence, and death. A few days later, Drake's mother received a telephone call telling her that her son had landed the coveted part. Sandi Graham remembers the moment well. "I called Aubrey and I asked him to come home, because we lived right across the street from the school at the time. He came home, and I told him, and of course he went crazy. He couldn't believe it."[17]

Originally, the producers of *Degrassi* had planned for Drake's character, Jimmy Brooks, to be a white football player. But they were so impressed with Drake's audition that they decided to make the character a black basketball

CHAPTER TWO

17

star. Tall, good looking, with a deep, expressive voice and a winning personality, Drake became an immediate fan favorite. Whenever the cast would make a personal appearance to promote the show, Drake would be mobbed by screaming fans—mostly girls. For Drake, who had earlier experienced so much rejection by the opposite sex, the turnaround was eye-opening. Many of his later raps would explore how fame makes a person more attractive but also how a star should be wary of those attracted by fame.

Rising Star

Drake emerged as one of the stars of *Degrassi*, earning a nomination for best supporting actor in a television series in 2005 from the Young Artist Association, a nonprofit organization founded to recognize and award excellence in youth performers. Impressed with Drake's acting skills, the producers of the series decided to make the most of Drake's talent by featuring him at the center of a plotline that would explore another important social issue: school shootings. In one episode, a bullied teen responds to the abuse he has received by bringing a gun to school and threatening Jimmy Brooks. Drake's character tries to escape from the gunman, but the classmate shoots him in the back. The gunshot wound leaves Jimmy paralyzed from the waist down.

Drake had to call on all of his skills to make Jimmy's plight believable. "I saw it as a challenge, so I did my research," Drake told MTV. "I actually took a kid that was in a wheelchair out and tried to understand how difficult it is to be mobile and live life as if nothing was wrong." To better understand the life experience of a wheelchair-bound person, Drake spent most of his workdays in a wheelchair, learning to use it more naturally so his character would seem real. The experience made Drake more sensitive to those who are physically challenged. "Playing Jimmy all day and being able to get up and walk away is weird," he said. "I appreciate things a lot more now."[18]

> "Playing Jimmy all day and being able to get up and walk away is weird. I appreciate things a lot more now."[18]
>
> —Drake

Drake became an instant fan favorite when he played the role of a star high school basketball player in the Canadian television series Degrassi: The Next Generation. Drake appears here (top, right) with other cast members in 2004.

Drake learned from his interaction with his wheelchair-bound friend that life—any life—is about the choices a person makes. "You start down at the bottom of the barrel, feeling loss emotionally. Then you rise up, slowly but surely, because you realize that, 'I could sit here, and could not live my life, and I could live in sorrow, or I could accept the cards I've been dealt.'"[19] Drake incorporated this insight into his portrayal of Jimmy. It was an acting choice that *Degrassi*'s executive producer Aaron Martin believes was extremely effective. "The great thing about Aubrey is that Aubrey never plays it like a victim," said Martin. "Aubrey, I don't think, ever could play it as a victim, because Aubrey is way too full of life. And he's put that into Jimmy very smartly, and that's been a very great decision on Aubrey's part—to portray Jimmy in a wheelchair with a zest for life."[20]

Drake's character began to do many things to cope with the pain of his disability, including drawing, writing, visiting art museums, and composing rap lyrics. Jimmy's shooting occurred in the fourth year of the program, when Drake was seventeen. By then he had been rapping with Poverty over the phone for several months. Rather than having the show's writers try to come up with raps for Jimmy, Drake offered to write them himself. He wrote all of the material he performed in the program. In less than a year, Drake went from performing raps for one lonely inmate to rapping for millions.

Dropout

Although *Degrassi* did not pay Drake huge sums of money, he was making a steady salary. This was a good thing for his family,

Encouragement from a Fan

Drake's performance as Jimmy Brooks impressed not only *Degrassi*'s producers and television critics but also the viewers. A fan named Jason took the time to express his appreciation in a letter to Drake. The young star was so touched by the fan's comments that he read parts of the letter aloud during the behind-the-scenes television program *Degrassi Unscripted* and thanked the fan on the air:

This is one of the nicest letters I've ever received from anybody. He feels that I can complete the trifecta of the greatest African American actors of all time—Sidney Poitier, Denzel Washington, and he says, "The third addition would be Aubrey Graham." Jason, I thank you, man. . . . I appreciate it with all my heart. Just know that I keep it close, and I will keep this with me for the rest of my life. No matter where I go, you're the one who said it. So, if it happens, it happens, man, you called it.

Quoted in *Degrassi Unscripted*, YouTube, November 5, 2018. https://youtu.be/RHxs3-dLh4k.

because his mother began suffering from rheumatoid arthritis, a painful disease of the joints. The arthritis became so bad that by the early 2000s she could no longer work, leaving Drake as the breadwinner of the family. "My mother was very sick," Drake recalls. "We were very poor, like broke. The only money I had coming in was off of Canadian TV, which isn't that much money when you break it down. A season of Canadian television is under a teacher's salary, I'll tell you that much."[21] It was, however, enough for the family to survive. "I had to become a man very quickly and be the backbone for a woman who I love with all my heart, my mother,"[22] he says.

With the success of his performance in *Degrassi*, Drake came to believe that his future was in show business. He also came to the conclusion that there was not much more he could learn in high school that would be useful in the career he was already pursuing full time. As a result, he decided to drop out of high school at age sixteen. It was a major life decision, although it did not seem so at the time. One day at school, Drake was arguing with a history teacher. Out of frustration, Drake picked up his backpack and walked toward the door. The teacher told him that if he left the classroom, he should not return. Drake took that as an excuse to do what he had been thinking about for a long time. He dropped out.

Drake's mother, a teacher, was not pleased with her son's decision. Drake later said that he did not regret dropping out but that he might go back to school to earn a diploma, which he would give to his mother. Ten years later he did just that, earning his final high school credits through correspondence courses. On October 18, 2012, Drake announced on Twitter: "97% on my final exam. 88% in the course. One of the greatest feelings in my entire life. As of tonight I have graduated high school!"[23]

"I had to become a man very quickly and be the backbone for a woman who I love with all my heart, my mother."[22]

—Drake

Performing in Public

Encouraged by his raps with Poverty and needing to earn extra money, Drake decided to form a band in 2003. He and his friend Dalton "D10" Tennant, a keyboardist, recruited two vocalists for the combo: Melanie Fiona and Aion Clark, who is also known as Voyce Alexander. Fiona, who would later win Grammy Awards for Best Traditional R&B Performance and Best R&B Song for the song "Fool for You" with CeeLo Green, already had a professional manager, Carmen Murray. Tennant played keyboards, Fiona and Clark sang, and Drake rapped.

The group, known as the Renaissance, specialized in hip-hop and R&B covers. The Renaissance performed songs made famous by John Legend, Alicia Keys, Etta James, and others. Drake covered various raps, including "Tainted" by Slum Village. Murray got

Canadian recording artist Melanie Fiona (shown performing in New York in 2018) was one of two vocalists who joined a new band formed by Drake and a friend in 2003. The band, known as the Renaissance, specialized in hip-hop and R&B covers.

Drake's Biggest Musical Influence

In his 2009 song "Say What's Real," Drake raps over background music produced by Kanye West for his 2008 song "Say You Will." The borrowed, or sampled, material includes a thumping drumbeat, two electronic bleeps—one high and one low—that alternate like the ticks of a clock, and a chorus of voices singing wordless notes in harmony. When Drake reissued the song in 2018, he credited West as the song's producer. In 2018 Drake said that West was the artist who had the greatest influence on his music:

> Before I ever got the chance to meet him, Kanye West shaped a lot of what I do, as far as music goes. We always, always, always took the time to listen to Kanye's music and appreciate it. . . . We searched the samples and we find out where his inspiration came from, because he has one of the best ears in music, period. He knows how to recognize great music that's not his. He knows how to utilize great sounds and great music. So before I met him, I had the utmost respect for Kanye West. I'd even go as far as to say he's the most influential person as far as a musician that I'd ever had in my life.

Quoted in Brianne Tracy, "From Joint Album Teases to Twitter Feuds: A Timeline of Drake and Kanye West's Relationship," *People*, December 17, 2018. https://people.com.

the Renaissance a regular gig at the Avocado Supper Club in downtown Toronto, a trendy night spot known for its celebrity clientele. In addition to rapping, Drake acted as emcee, introducing songs and interacting with the audience. The act was a big success.

Drake's involvement with the Renaissance came to an end one night when he received a call from Murray. He remembers the call word for word: "She was like, I'm sorry, I hate to be the one to do this, but I just got to tell you, you're out of the group. I don't think music is your calling." Drake was stunned. "My heart dropped. I was shocked when I got kicked out. I was like the

OG [original] member."[24] Drake was wounded, but he did not give up on his dream of being a professional musician. Instead, he worked harder than ever to make his raps flow, eventually developing a sound that would one day take him to the top of the charts.

Actor by Day, Emcee by Night

The celebrity status Drake gained from *Degrassi* and from his short-lived stint with the Renaissance brought him into contact with other people in show business in Toronto. Several of these performers and producers were members of the Toronto hip-hop scene. After shooting for *Degrassi* would finish for the day, Drake would often visit the recording studios of his new friends, composing lyrics to the beats they would play and recording his raps on their equipment.

Proud of his musical creations, Drake began to upload them to his fan page on the social media platform Myspace. Most of the visitors to his Myspace page were fans of *Degrassi*, but many enjoyed seeing a different side to one of their favorite actors. Encouraged by the response to his music, in 2006 Drake created his first mixtape—a recording that includes sections of well-known songs, known as samples, with the recording artist, or emcee, rapping over their beats. The mixtape, *Room for Improvement*, was a compilation of twenty-two songs—seventeen of Drake's raps plus music by others. To separate his musical endeavors from his acting career, he released the mixtape under his middle name, Drake. It was the name he would use from then on in the music industry.

Drake began to spend more and more time making music. As soon as his work on *Degrassi* was finished, he would head to a recording studio nearby. "Back then, I'd spend a full day on set and then go to the studio to make music until 4 or 5 a.m.," he recalls. "I'd sleep in my dressing room and then be in front of the cameras again by 9 a.m." Word got around about Drake's late-night activities, and the producers of *Degrassi* became concerned. "Eventually, they realized I was juggling two professions and told me I had to choose. I chose this life," he says, referring to his musical career. In 2008 the producers of *Degrassi* decided to revamp the series. Drake, who was then twenty-two, was told he would no longer be one of the regular cast members. After seven years of receiving a small but steady paycheck, the young actor-musician suddenly was without an income. "I was coming to terms with the fact that, okay, people know me from 'Degrassi,' but I might have to work at a restaurant or something just to keep things going," he remembers. "The money from that show was very small. And it was dwindling."[25]

Drake had lost his job, but not his dream. He wanted to forge a career as a musician. His television career had given him a platform to make that dream come true. Because of *Degrassi*, he had a fan base. He was known by celebrities in the television and music industries. He was also known by a large number of people in the entertainment media. Such notoriety does not last forever, however, especially if a person is not in the spotlight. With *Degrassi* behind him, he knew he had to act quickly if Drake was to become as well known as Aubrey Graham.

> "Eventually, they realized I was juggling two professions and told me I had to choose. I chose this life."[25]
>
> —Drake

SELF-PRODUCED STARDOM

For decades the only way for a musician to reach a mass audience was to sign a contract with a record label. The label would release the artist's recordings on records, tapes, or CDs to the public. The labels would also promote the recordings to commercial radio stations that played new music. By the twenty-first century, however, that whole picture was changing. Artists were going straight to the people by posting digital files of their music on social media pages, blogs, or their own websites. They were building a following without the backing of a record label. This is the route Drake took with his music. The move paid off. He received so much attention from his self-produced music that several traditional record labels got involved in a bidding war to begin producing his future work.

Drake did not build his following all by himself. He had the help of a core group of music professionals in Toronto. One of these was Toronto hip-hop artist Promise, who had released a studio album in 2002. Promise advised Drake to start a Myspace page so he could make his music available to the public. Promise also gave him his first access to a professional recording studio, which improved the sound of Drake's recordings. "I was amazed at how well he wrote for someone who wasn't actually an artist," Promise recalls. "So I encouraged him to keep writing and invited him to my studio, where he recorded his first hits that later ended up on his *Room for Improvement* mixtape."[26] Other members of the Toronto hip-hop scene that Drake got to know included Matthew "Boi-1da" Samuels, who produced three of the songs on *Room for Improvement*; Slakah the Beatchild, who featured the young Drake on his 2008 album,

Soul Movement Vol. 1; and DJ Smallz, who hosted Drake's debut mixtape. These local artists and producers helped Drake hone his skills and make a splash with *Room for Improvement*. Through their combined efforts, the mixtape sold about six thousand copies from Drake's Myspace page.

Breaking Into the US Market

Gaining thousands of fans for his music was no small achievement, but Drake had bigger ambitions. He wanted to break into the US music market, which has far more rap and hip-hop fans, critics, and media outlets than the Canadian market. To accomplish this ambitious feat, Drake needed to reach out beyond his inner circle to tastemakers in the United States. One of these was Terral "Hollaback" T. Slack, the chief executive officer of the artist management firm Bigger Picture Entertainment. Slack, who already represented Boi-1da, was skeptical about the young actor-turned-rapper, but he changed his mind when he listened to Drake's mixtape. "I use to rock with one of DJ Smallz' people real heavy," Slack recalls. He continues:

> **"She sent me the music and I said, "This kid is dope!""**[27]
>
> —Terral "Hollaback" T. Slack, chief executive officer of Bigger Picture Entertainment

> She was telling me about this cat named Drake on "Degrassi", you know. I was like, "What . . . is Degrassi?" because I never heard of it. She was like, "He is on this teen TV show." So I was like, "Cool, whatever." I kind of brushed it off. Then she sent me the music and I said, "This kid is dope! What's the situation? What's going on?" So she put us on 3-way [phone call], and the rest is history.[27]

After signing Drake to his firm, Slack put his team to work on the Toronto rapper's Myspace page, instructing them to respond to each and every message Drake received. This helped drive the number of Drake's followers from 30,000 to more than 1 million in

A core group of music professionals in the Toronto hip-hop scene helped Drake build a following. One them was producer Matthew "Boi-1da" Samuels (shown here at a 2019 performance in Los Angeles).

less than a year. The surge in followers led Myspace to name Drake the most-followed musician without a recording contract in 2007. Slack also brought Drake to the attention of major media outlets, including the hip-hop publications *XXL* and *Source*, and Sirius Satellite Radio's hip-hop channel Shade 45. The growing attention to Drake as a musician allowed Slack to seek out established collaborators for Drake's second mixtape, *Comeback Season*.

Teaming Up with Trey Songz

One of the artists Drake most wanted to work with was the R&B singer Trey Songz. Drake was working on a particular song when he realized Songz was the ideal artist to sing the song's hook, a short musical phrase that is used to make a song appealing and catch the attention of the listener. Drake sent the unfinished song to Slack, who forwarded it to Songz through one of his connections. The R&B artist liked what he heard and invited Drake to Atlanta to meet face-to-face. The two got along well, and Songz laid down vocal tracks for the song that would become known as "Replacement Girl."

In the song, Drake raps for the first sixty seconds about his lifestyle as a musician. The only musical accompaniment to the rap is a bass guitar and finger snaps. Drake then announces that the album is for his fans, but the hook is for his ex-girlfriends. Songz then croons the melodic hook, still accompanied only by a bass guitar and finger snaps but with the addition of backup singers and synthesized keyboard. Songz then sings a new verse, reminiscent of the soul music Drake had grown up listening to, and repeats the hook. This smooth, laid-back section of the song lasts for about ninety seconds. Drake raps for another thirty seconds before Songz returns, singing the hook one more time. The blend of rap lyrics with an R&B hook would be a form that Drake would return to through his career, until it became his signature sound.

The reaction to the song was so positive that Drake decided to feature it in a music video. In the video, Drake and Songz appear side by side in front of an oversized map of the world and beside a car, while interacting with various female dancers. Slack promoted the video to all of the major US outlets. Black Entertainment Television (BET) aired it on its top-rated program, *106 & Park*, a show that counted down the top hip-hop and R&B videos of the day. It was the first time in BET's twenty-seven-year history that the network featured a debut video by a Canadian rapper with no record contract. The video debuted on April 30, 2007, as "New Joint of the Day" and was voted by the show's fans onto the top-ten chart. MTV also added the video to its rotation, and urban radio stations played the song.

An Important Contact

"Replacement Girl" brought Drake to the attention of hip-hop fans in the United States, but another track on *Comeback Season*, "Man of the Year," had a bigger impact on Drake's career. It did so by coming to the attention of just one person: rapper and music

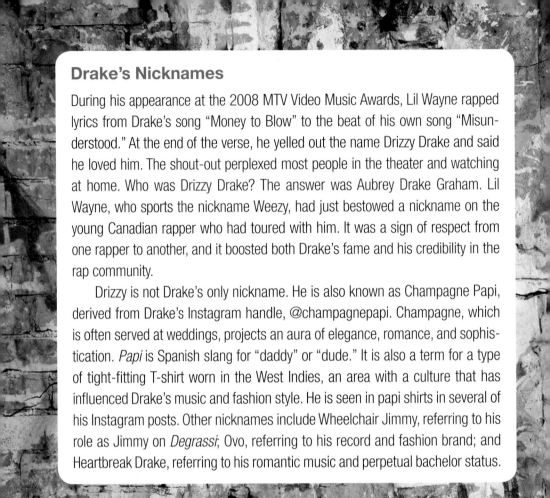

Drake's Nicknames

During his appearance at the 2008 MTV Video Music Awards, Lil Wayne rapped lyrics from Drake's song "Money to Blow" to the beat of his own song "Misunderstood." At the end of the verse, he yelled out the name Drizzy Drake and said he loved him. The shout-out perplexed most people in the theater and watching at home. Who was Drizzy Drake? The answer was Aubrey Drake Graham. Lil Wayne, who sports the nickname Weezy, had just bestowed a nickname on the young Canadian rapper who had toured with him. It was a sign of respect from one rapper to another, and it boosted both Drake's fame and his credibility in the rap community.

Drizzy is not Drake's only nickname. He is also known as Champagne Papi, derived from Drake's Instagram handle, @champagnepapi. Champagne, which is often served at weddings, projects an aura of elegance, romance, and sophistication. *Papi* is Spanish slang for "daddy" or "dude." It is also a term for a type of tight-fitting T-shirt worn in the West Indies, an area with a culture that has influenced Drake's music and fashion style. He is seen in papi shirts in several of his Instagram posts. Other nicknames include Wheelchair Jimmy, referring to his role as Jimmy on *Degrassi*; Ovo, referring to his record and fashion brand; and Heartbreak Drake, referring to his romantic music and perpetual bachelor status.

executive Lil Wayne. On the track, Drake samples "Man of the Year" by Brisco, Flo Rida, and Lil Wayne. The track opens with Drake rapping for ninety seconds over the same beat used in Lil Wayne's song. Drake then includes Lil Wayne's opening rap, which is about twenty seconds long. Drake raps again and then drops in Lil Wayne's verse for a second time. Music producer James "Jas" Prince, who had chatted with Drake on Myspace and knew Lil Wayne, enjoyed the mixtape. He thought Lil Wayne might like to hear how Drake had used his song, so he gave Lil Wayne a copy of "Man of the Year" as a gift. Lil Wayne was so impressed with Drake's effort that he called the young rapper from Prince's phone. Drake later said that he thought the call was a prank:

I think Wayne called me when I was in the barbershop getting my hair cut. He called me from [Jas's] phone so I thought it was [Jas]. I picked up and I heard a completely different voice, I knew the voice right away but I didn't wanna believe it so I'm like, "Whatever, man." And he's like, "Yo, this is Weezy," and I'm [sarcastically] like, "Yeah, aight [alright]." He's like, "Yo, this is Weezy, can you get on a plane by tomorrow at 8:00am?"[28]

Drake immediately accepted the invitation to meet one of his music idols. He flew to Houston, where Lil Wayne invited him to join his 2008–2009 I Am Music Tour. Appearing with Lil Wayne

Lil Wayne (left) and Drake perform together in 2011 in Los Angeles. When Lil Wayne invited Drake to join his 2008–2009 I Am Music Tour, Drake happily accepted. He relished the chance to perform with one of his music idols.

and rapping his new lyrics to Lil Wayne's well-known hit brought Drake to the attention of fans and industry insiders alike. More importantly, as Drake and Lil Wayne toured together, they collaborated on several new songs. Drake later put these collaborations on his third self-produced mixtape, *So Far Gone*. Lil Wayne's guest appearance on four of Drake's songs gave Drake instant credibility in the rap and hip-hop world. People knew Lil Wayne would not collaborate with someone if he did not think that person was up to his standards.

Lil Wayne's involvement with *So Far Gone* helped Drake in another way. It made it easier for him to recruit other well-known performers to also collaborate on his mixtape. Other guest artists who added vocals to the mixtape include Omarion, Lloyd, Lykke Li, and Bun B. Trey Songz teamed up with Drake again, singing the hook of the song "Successful." Drake rapped three verses of the song, and Lil Wayne rapped the final verse.

Breaking onto the Music Charts

Rather than charge for the mixtape, Drake made it available for free on his own website in September 2009. The mixtape received more than two thousand downloads in its first two hours. It also began receiving radio play. Critics gave it favorable reviews. Guido Stern of RapReviews.com gave *So Far Gone* 9.5 out a possible 10 points for both "Music Vibes" and "Lyric Vibes." Stern writes, "'So Far Gone' is unquestionably one of the most cohesive, atmospheric hip hop records in recent memory—which is almost the antithesis of what one expects from a mixtape. Drake is not a gangster rapper and never goes down that path, instead proving how many ways there are to cleverly rap about problematic relationships and being on the verge of stardom."[29]

The mainstream media also gave Drake favorable reviews. *Boston Globe*

> "'So Far Gone' is unquestionably one of the most cohesive, atmospheric hip hop records in recent memory."[29]
>
> —Guido Stern, music reviewer for RapReviews.com

The Man Behind YOLO

Beginning in late 2011, a new word swept across North America: *YOLO*, meaning "you only live once." YOLO began to appear in Twitter hashtags, on Instagram, and elsewhere in late October 2011. On December 16, 2011, the *Huffington Post* published a photo of the American actor Zac Efron with YOLO tattooed on the side of his right hand. The word became so prevalent that when President Barack Obama made a public service announcement promoting his signature health care plan in 2015, he ended the lighthearted spot with the words "YOLO, Man."

The word's sudden appearance made many people wonder where it had come from. A data analytics tool used to track keywords on Twitter showed that tweets using "YOLO" spiked starting on October 24, 2011. One day before, Drake had posted a tweet with the words "YOLO" and "you only live once" along with a picture of himself standing on a balcony. The tweet was a teaser for his song "The Motto," which debuted on October 31, 2011. In the song's hook, Drake says that You Only Live Once is the motto that he and his friends live by. "The Motto" reached number one on both the Hot R&B/Hip-Hop Songs and US Rap Songs charts. In December 2011, when Walgreens advertised hats emblazoned with YOLO on the front, Drake tweeted that it should either pull the headgear off the shelves or pay him a royalty for using the word he had popularized. Nothing came of his comment.

Quoted in Betsy Klein, "President Barack Obama: 'YOLO Man,'" CNN, February 12, 2015. https://edition.cnn.com.

critic Julian Benbow praised Drake's "soft touches of humor and honesty," explaining, "those girls love his Rolls Royce Phantom, he says on 'Successful,' even if it's leased. The soft touches go satin, though, on 'Brand New' and 'Sooner Than Later,' where Drake shows symptoms of a full-blown R&B singer. 'So Far Gone' makes it obvious that Drake is multidimensional, but his words sound best when he's telling his own story."[30]

For the first time in Drake's career, one of his songs cracked the *Billboard* Hot 100 chart. "Best I Ever Had" spent twenty-four weeks on the *Billboard* Hot 100 chart, peaking at number two behind the megahit "I Gotta Feeling" by the Black Eyed Peas. "Best I Ever Had" went on to top both the *Billboard* Hot R&B/Hip-Hop Songs chart and the *Billboard* Rap Songs chart, giving Drake his first number one hit on both of these charts. The second single from *So Far Gone*, "Successful," also enjoyed chart success, reaching number seventeen on the *Billboard* Hot 100, number two on the *Billboard* Rap Songs chart, and number three on the Hot R&B/Hip-Hop Songs chart.

The success of these songs prompted Drake to release five songs from the mixtape plus two new songs as an extended play recording, or EP. Sold, rather than made available for free, the EP debuted at number six on the *Billboard* 200 album chart. It went on to win Rap Recording of the Year at the 2010 Juno Awards,

Drake accepts one of his two 2010 Juno Awards from the Canadian Academy of Recording Arts and Sciences. He received one award for New Artist of the Year and the other for Rap Recording of the Year for So Far Gone.

presented by the Canadian Academy of Recording Arts and Sciences for achievements by Canadian musical artists.

Bidding War

Drake had accomplished all of this success without the backing of a record company. He had taken his work directly to the people via the Internet and forged collaborations with A-list performers and music producers through the personal efforts of his team. No independent artist had ever achieved so much on his or her own. The major record labels, including Universal Motown Records, Atlantic Records, and Warner Music Group, took notice of the young rapper's success and entered into what *Rolling Stone* magazine called one of the biggest bidding wars ever in hopes of signing Drake. *Rolling Stone* reported that at least one of the labels offered Drake $2 million up front to persuade the young artist to join its roster.

In the end loyalty was more important to Drake than money. Lil Wayne was the first big name to recognize his talent, and his collaborations with Drake were largely responsible for the success of *So Far Gone*. Drake announced that he had signed with Lil Wayne's company, Young Money Entertainment. "When it gets to a certain point you need the machine that is a label," Drake explains. "And we got on that scale thanks to Wayne. Wayne did a lot for me from the very early stages. The foresight he had just meant the world to me, the biggest sign of respect that I've ever had. So the choice [as to which record label to sign to] . . . it was a no-brainer to me."[31] With a contract from a major hip-hop record label in hand, Drake had arrived.

CHART TOPPER

Once Drake received the backing of a major record label, he enjoyed unprecedented chart success. He released five studio albums and three mixtapes in eight years, all of which debuted at number one on the *Billboard* 200. Nearly two hundred of his songs broke into the *Billboard* Hot 100 singles chart. The sheer volume of Drake's work is impressive, and no matter how many songs he releases, his fans clamor for more. Some music critics are not as enthusiastic about his massive output. They fault Drake for saying a lot without having a lot to say. Following the monumental success of Drake's 2018 single "God's Plan," which logged more than 200 million streams in just three weeks, one music critic suggested that Drake should only release material when he has something fresh and important to say. He wrote, "If Drake were smart, he would take the enormous success of 'God's Plan' as a sign and stop releasing albums altogether."[32]

Auspicious Debut

Drake's first album for Lil Wayne's Young Money Entertainment, *Thank Me Later*, was released in 2010. It debuted at number one on the *Billboard* 200, selling more than 447,000 copies in its first week. The immediate success of the album was due in part to the success of four singles that were released before the album dropped, creating anticipation for the full album. The first single, "Over," topped the *Billboard* Rap Songs chart and was nominated for Best Rap Solo Performance at the 53rd Annual Grammy Awards. The second single, "Find Your Love," also went to number one on the Rap Songs chart. The third and fourth singles, "Miss Me" and "Fancy," were moderate hits, but "Fancy," which featured vocals from rappers T.I. and Swizz Beatz, earned Drake a second Grammy nomination for Best Rap Performance by a Duo or Group.

Although *Thank Me Later* was a commercial success, Drake was not entirely pleased with the album. He felt its production was rushed, and he believed he could have improved many of his lyrics if he had taken more time. In addition, the album's tracks were created by several different high-profile producers as a way of increasing interest in the work. As a result, the album did not have a cohesive sound. "I think I got caught up in making it seem big and first-album-ish," he told *Rolling Stone*. "I was a bit numb, a bit disconnected from myself. I wasn't able to slow down and realize what was going on around me." Drake decided to take more time putting together his next album—a fact reflected by the 2011 album's title, *Take Care*. "The whole process has been about slowing life down and really pinpointing emotions,"[33] he said.

> "The whole process has been about slowing life down and really pinpointing emotions."[33]
>
> —Drake

Things were happening that were causing him to reflect more deeply on his personal life. His mother, who had been battling health issues, suddenly needed surgery in July 2010. Drake was on tour in Europe when he received the news. He canceled the rest of his tour to be at his mother's side and support her through her recovery. The sudden illness made Drake reflect on how stardom was affecting his private life. In the song "Resistance," he describes how a longtime friend told him that she missed the old Drake. He admits in the song that he had just learned that his grandmother had been put into a nursing home and that he had not called her. Instead, he had just called a young woman he had met at the mall. He wonders aloud when his old self went missing.

Critical Success

Drake released four singles ahead of *Take Care*, all four of which topped the *Billboard* Hot Rap Songs, making Drake the artist with the most number one singles in the history of the chart. *Take Care* debuted at number one on the *Billboard* 200, selling 631,000

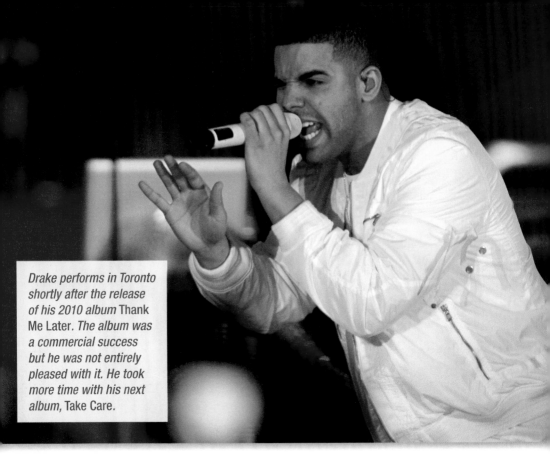

Drake performs in Toronto shortly after the release of his 2010 album Thank Me Later. *The album was a commercial success but he was not entirely pleased with it. He took more time with his next album,* Take Care.

copies in its first week of sales. It also topped the US Top R&B/ Hip-Hop Albums and Top Rap Albums charts. It ended 2012 as the third-best-selling album of the year.

On *Take Care*, Drake began to sing his own hooks, rather than relying on other singers to do so. His practice of alternately rapping and singing came to define his sound. The album was a critical success. "*Take Care* is full of gorgeous tones: atmospheric, moody, muted music that can turn suddenly gushing and lavish," wrote Nitsuh Abebe of *New York* magazine. "And the lyrics surrounding them can be rich with meaning, like on 'Look What You've Done,' which begins with Drake rapping about taking care of his ill mother."[34] Evan Rytlewski of AV Club was also impressed. "[*Take Care*] is plenty downbeat," he wrote, "but it's also gorgeous, an immersive headphone masterwork that's tender and intimate like little else in contemporary rap and R&B."[35] *Take Care* won the Grammy Award for Best Rap Album at the 55th Annual Grammy Awards.

Determined to Improve

In a pattern that repeated itself with each album, Drake said that while he was proud of his last album, he felt he could do better. This was not just hype to promote his forthcoming album, *Nothing Was the Same*. A young artist who was still developing his talents, Drake was serious about wanting to improve. "*Take Care* is a great album, but I listened to it and realized where I could do better and I think I've done better on this album," he told MTV News. "The music that I'm making is more concise, more clear, and I've been able to get my thoughts a lot better on this album." Drake said he was inspired by the soul singer Marvin Gaye, who was known for singing not only love songs but also social commentary. "I have aspirations to be Marvin Gaye in the back of my head," Drake said. "I just want to sing the world's triumphs and problems on one record."[36]

> "I just want to sing the world's triumphs and problems on one record."[36]
>
> —Drake

Many critics found that Drake had succeeded in his attempt to break new ground in the music world. "Drake wants to hold the spot as an innovator, and his signature style is grasping onto newer territories every day, influencing artists in the rap world and beyond," writes Eric Diep of *XXL*. "With the themes, moods and issues displayed here, Drizzy has shared another moment of his life, and now the only thing left to prove is if his crossover powers can last him a decade from now."[37] Drake's attempt to honor Marvin Gaye also succeeded. "'Hold On, We're Going Home' is the album's emotional centerpiece," writes Bryant Kitching of Consequence of Sound. "In a croon that'd give Marvin Gaye chills, Drake assures, 'I want your . . . emotion, endlessly.' There's no rapping at all here, and Drake's singing has never sounded better."[38] Released on September 24, 2013, *Nothing Was the Same* was a hit with fans as well, selling 658,000 copies in its first week of release. It was Drake's second straight album to debut at number one on the *Billboard* 200.

Drake's next five releases—*If You're Reading This It's Too Late*, *What a Time to Be Alive*, *Views*, *More Life*, and *Scorpion*—all

Drake Announces New Album

On April 9, 2019, Drake told the crowd at the London stop of his Assassination Vacation Tour that he had begun work on his next album. "I kinda actually started last night to be honest with you," he said. "But I think what I'm gonna do after this is I'm gonna go home, and I'm gonna make a new album so I can come back to London next year and we can do this again."

Industry insiders say that Drake has been working on new music with a number of artists, including American rappers Travis Scott and French Montana. In February 2019 Drake released a remix of R&B singer Summer Walker's song "Girls Need Love," leading some to wonder if the new album would include a collaboration with her as well. The entertainment website Top 40 reported in April 2019 that Drake might also be collaborating on new music with Ariana Grande, after the two suddenly began following each other on Instagram.

Since the unnamed album will be Drake's sixth, many people expect the album title to somehow include the number six. The number is associated with Drake, since he popularized "the Six," often written "the 6IX," as a nickname for Toronto. Not only did Drake originally plan to call his fourth studio album *Views from the 6*, but six is also the number on the Toronto Raptors basketball jersey that Drake sometimes wears as an official ambassador for the NBA team.

Quoted in Ben Myers, "Drake Tells London Audience He's Working on New Album," YouTube, April 11, 2019. https://youtu.be/ybKSDK6jawl.

debuted at number one on the *Billboard* 200 charts. Three of them—*If You're Reading This It's Too Late*, *What a Time to Be Alive*, and *More Life*—were mixtapes, while *Views* and *Scorpion* were studio albums. *What a Time to Be Alive* is a collaboration between Drake and American rapper Future.

Growing Criticism

Drake again challenged himself to make his next studio album better than his last. He planned the work to be a concept album centered in Toronto. The songs suggested the passing of seasons in Canada. He would call the album *Views from the 6*, referring to the six boroughs of Toronto that merged into one large city in 1998. In late 2015 he returned to Toronto from Southern California (where he had purchased a home) to write and record the winter section of the album in his hometown. The album cover shows a digitally altered image of Drake sitting on Toronto's CN Tower, the tallest free-standing structure in the Western Hemisphere. Drake's ambitions were high. When an interviewer asked how he thought the album would be received, Drake said, "I don't want you to get it right away. . . . Great music takes a little work. It takes elevating your listening level."[39]

The 2016 album, its title shortened to *Views*, received a lot of attention. The promotional efforts included an appearance by Drake on the comedy program *Saturday Night Live*. *Views* spent thirteen weeks at number one on the *Billboard* 200 chart.

The album cover for *Views* shows a digitally altered image of Drake sitting on Toronto's CN Tower (pictured). The album focuses on scenes and images of his hometown.

Reviews, however, were mixed. Some critics praised the danceable songs as some of Drake's best work in that genre. But most critics found that the album's twenty tracks included more weak songs than strong ones. "'VIEWS' is long. Very long. Very, very long. Twenty songs long. Nearly an hour and a half long," writes music critic Elliott Sharp. "For those who love Drake a whole lot, this longness will feel like heaven. But for those who think Drake's brand of self-indulgent yacht rap is excruciating in even small doses, 'VIEWS' might feel like hell."[40]

Drake's self-reflective songs, which critics found interesting in his first albums, began to seem repetitive to some. "Rarely has one man moaned quite so much about so little," writes Andy Gill of British newspaper the *Independent*. "Over 80 interminable minutes, the Canadian rapper appears to find no satisfaction in anything at all. . . . The overall effect is utterly wearying, and unpersuasive: after all, only fools waste pity on the wealthy."[41] Pitchfork's Ryan Dombal also found the album too long, but he said the real problem is the amount of time Drake spends complaining about his life. "There is a razor-sharp line between self-awareness and self-absorption," writes Dombal. "For the past seven years, Drake has expertly glided along that line. But on his fourth proper album, he edges closer than ever to a mirrored abyss, a suffocating echo chamber of self."[42]

Stung by the criticism, Drake spent two years working on his next album, using everything he had learned about recording to make his next album a commercial and critical success. He amassed a platoon of thirty-two different producers to work on the album's twenty-five tracks. He brought in rap superstar Jay-Z for a guest appearance on one track and included a recording of the late Michael Jackson on another. He used the services of twenty-one other guest vocalists. He sampled twenty-one songs performed by a range of artists, including Lil Wayne, Nas, Lauren Hill, N.W.A., Aaliyah, Nicki Minaj, Mariah Carey, Boyz II Men, and Marvin Gaye. He broke the massive eighty-nine-minute album into two parts—one featuring mostly rap and one featuring mostly R&B singing—to give it a clear structure.

The album, entitled *Scorpion*, dropped on June 29, 2018. It was preceded by the release of three interest-building singles, including Drake's biggest hit, "God's Plan." The single, backed by a video that shows Drake giving away $996,631 of the video's budget in cash to needy individuals and nonprofit organizations, debuted at number one on the *Billboard* Hot 100 and set records for first-day streaming on both Spotify and Apple Music. Powered by the success of "God's Plan," *Scorpion* logged a mind-boggling

At the 2019 Grammy Awards, Drake accepts the Best Rap Song Award for "God's Plan." That song appeared on the Scorpion album, which logged 1 billion streams in its first week but earned mixed reviews.

1 billion streams in its first week, shattering one-day records on streaming platforms Spotify and Apple Music in the process. To date, it is the most streamed album in history.

Most critics found *Scorpion* to be a big improvement over *Views*. "This is a revealing, thrilling album by an artist who took a very particular experience and used it to create a beautiful project,"[43] commented Tommy Monroe of Quietus. Mikael Wood of the *Los Angeles Times* noted the double album's extreme length but concluded, "'Scorpion' is so beautifully rendered—from vocals to samples to features to beats—that Drake ends up pulling you over to his side."[44] Other critics were not as forgiving. Jonny Coleman of the *Hollywood Reporter* called *Scorpion* "a double decker of obese proportions." Coleman continued, "*Scorpion* is proof that Drake has no editor and no distinct worldview. In trying to

> "'Scorpion' is so beautifully rendered—from vocals to samples to features to beats—that Drake ends up pulling you over to his side."[44]
>
> —Mikael Wood, *Los Angeles Times* music critic

Billboard Awards Record

On May 1, 2019, Drake set a record for the most career *Billboard* Music Awards. He received twelve awards, bringing his total to twenty-seven, surpassing Taylor Swift and her twenty-three career wins.

The twelve awards tied Drake with Adele for the second-most awards won in one year. He fell one award short of tying his own record of winning thirteen *Billboard* Music Awards in one year, a feat he accomplished in 2017 following the release of his fourth album, *Views*. His 2019 haul reflected the success of his fifth studio album, *Scorpion*, which won the award for Top *Billboard* 200 Album.

Drake also won 2019 *Billboard* Music Awards for Top Artist, Top Male Artist, Top Streaming Artist, Top *Billboard* 200 Artist, Top Radio Songs Artist, Top Hot 100 Artist, Top Song Sales Artist, Top Rap Artist, Top Rap Male Artist, Top Rap Album for *Scorpion*, and Top Streaming Song for "In My Feelings."

please too many people—rap heads, soccer moms and everyone in between—he's lost a sense of himself."[45]

Drake's fans had mixed feelings as well. *Scorpion* debuted at number one on the *Billboard* 200 chart, selling 732,000 album-equivalent units. However, that total lagged an incredible 692,000 units behind the first-week sales of *Views*. In fact, *Scorpion* had the lowest first-week sales of any album in Drake's career. Nevertheless, it remained at number one for five consecutive weeks and ended the year as the second-best-selling album of the year. In addition, *Scorpion* and its singles also received recognition from the music awards community. *Scorpion* was nominated for Album of the Year at the 2019 Grammy Awards. In addition, its blockbuster single, "God's Plan," was nominated for Record of the Year, Song of the Year, and Best Rap Song, the last of which it won. *Scorpion* won Top *Billboard* 200 Album at the 2019 *Billboard* Music Awards, one of twelve awards Drake received related to the album.

On August 2, 2019, Drake released his first compilation album, *Care Package*. The album consists of seventeen songs recorded from 2010 to 2016 that were never before available for purchase or commercial streaming. *Care Package* debuted at number one on the *Billboard* 200, joining Drake's five studio albums and three of his mixtapes to become his ninth number one recording on the chart. The album spawned six new *Billboard* Hot 100 singles, bringing Drake's career total to 203. In what was otherwise a quiet year for Drake, *Care Package* showed that he was still one of the biggest stars in the recording industry.

BRANCHING OUT

When Drake was seventeen, he told *Degrassi Unscripted* that music and acting were the only things he could commit to in his life. The young television star knew himself well. For two decades he has made a career out of those two endeavors. His acting career helped him launch his music career, and his music career has opened doors for more acting. In addition, Drake's global fame and personal wealth have enabled him to explore business and philanthropic interests. Now in his thirties, Drake is branching out.

October's Very Own

Even before Drake became famous, he was involved in the production side of the music business. He released his first self-produced mixtape, *Room for Improvement*, on his own All Things Fresh record label. Drake released his next two mixtapes, *Comeback Season* and *So Far Gone*, on a label he called October's Very Own, a name derived from a blog page he and his partner Oliver El-Khatib launched in April 2008. October's Very Own is a reference to Drake's birth month and that of several of his friends. Buoyed by the success of *So Far Gone*, Drake launched a music festival in Toronto that coincided with Canada's Civic Holiday weekend. Drake shortened the name October's Very Own to OVO to create the festival name: OVO Fest. When Drake teamed up with music producer Noah "40" Shebib and El-Khatib to launch a record label in 2012, they called it OVO Sound.

OVO Sound has released three of Drake's mixtapes, produced in partnership with Young Money Entertainment, Republic Records, and other labels. OVO Sound is also one of the labels behind Drake's third studio album, *Nothing Was the Same*. Wanting to help other struggling artists in the same way that Lil Wayne had helped him, Drake has signed nine other recording artists to OVO Sound. These artists have produced a total of twenty-one commercial releases. Two OVO Sound albums have been certified platinum or higher by the RIAA.

OVO Clothing

Also in 2011, Drake, Shebib, and El-Khatib launched a line of clothing to capitalize on Drake's growing fame. They named the company OVO Clothing. The company's logo is an owl drawn with simple, gold lines. OVO Clothing teamed up with clothing manufacturer Canada Goose to create parkas and jackets that appeal to Drake's sense of style. In 2015 the company partnered with Nike to produce Drake's own collection of Air Jordan athletic shoes, known as Air Jordan OVOs. Drake takes the clothing line seriously. "I want people to be a part of our movement, I just want it to be right," he says. "And everybody else wants me to make it with the cheaper fabric and put it in Macy's and 'Oh don't worry we will make 100 million in the first year.' Naw, . . . that's not what we are about. I'm not ready for OVO to be that. Because OVO is still something I represent."[46]

> "Everybody else wants me to make it with the cheaper fabric and put it in Macy's. . . . I'm not ready for OVO to be that. Because OVO is still something I represent."[46]
>
> —Drake

OVO Clothing opened its first branded clothing boutique in Toronto in 2014. It now has retail outlets in New York, Los Angeles, and London. In addition to parkas and jackets, the company offers hoodies, knit beanies, T-shirts, beach towels, keychains, notebooks, water bottles, phone covers, and more—all branded with the golden OVO owl. The online publication the *Business of Fashion* estimates that OVO Clothing's annual sales reached $50 million in 2018.

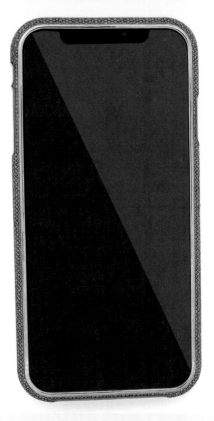

Drake and his business partners have launched several businesses including a record label and clothing line—all under the name OVO. Drake's diamond studded iPhone case features a white gold owl, which is the company's logo.

Toronto Raptors Ambassador

Drake's knowledge of fashion, branding, and culture led him to become a brand consultant to the Toronto Raptors of the NBA. In 2013 Drake formally joined the executive committee of the Raptors in the role of global ambassador for the team. He played a prominent role in Toronto's successful bid to host the 2016 NBA All-Star Game, and he served as the host of the All-Star Game festivities. He provides consulting to the team regarding its clothing line, and he is often seen at Raptors games wearing Raptors gear. He has a courtside seat at Raptors home games, where he cheers on the team. When the Raptors are on the road, Drake sometimes shows up at Jurassic Park, the Raptors fans' nickname for the public square adjacent to the Raptors' home arena, where fans gather to watch games on large-screen televisions. Using a mic connected to a sound system, Drake talks to the crowd, leads the cheering from a stage, and sometimes raps and sings in concert with the fans, many of whom know his lyrics by heart.

Drake's passion for the Raptors became controversial in May 2019, when the Toronto team was playing the Milwaukee Bucks in the NBA's Eastern Conference Finals. In the fourth game of the series, with Toronto down two games to one, Drake repeatedly mingled with Raptors players during time-outs, cheering them on. At one point he spontaneously gave Raptors coach Nick Nurse a quick shoulder rub. After the game, which the Raptors won, Bucks coach Mike Budenholzer complained about Drake's courtside behavior. "There's certainly no place for fans and, you know, whatever it is exactly that Drake is for the Toronto Raptors," Budenholzer said in conference call with ESPN. "You know, to be on the court, there's boundaries and lines for a reason, and like I said, the league is usually pretty good at being on top of stuff like that."[47] Drake responded the next day by posting a picture on Instagram that showed him celebrating the Raptors' win on the court. In the picture's comments area, Drake posted three sarcastic emojis: a

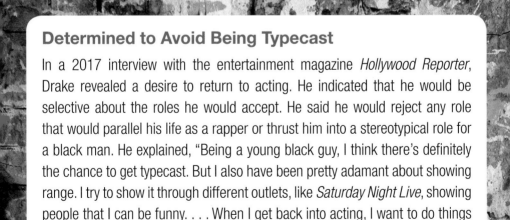

Determined to Avoid Being Typecast

In a 2017 interview with the entertainment magazine *Hollywood Reporter*, Drake revealed a desire to return to acting. He indicated that he would be selective about the roles he would accept. He said he would reject any role that would parallel his life as a rapper or thrust him into a stereotypical role for a black man. He explained, "Being a young black guy, I think there's definitely the chance to get typecast. But I also have been pretty adamant about showing range. I try to show it through different outlets, like *Saturday Night Live*, showing people that I can be funny. . . . When I get back into acting, I want to do things that make people go, 'Wow, I didn't expect that.'"

Tatiana Siegel, "Drake's Hotline to Hollywood: Inside an Ambitious Push into Film and TV," *Hollywood Reporter*, November 8, 2017. www.hollywoodreporter.com.

laughing face, a salt shaker (indicating when someone is being "salty," or angry), and a man shrugging. The emojis suggest that Drake did not take the coach's comments too seriously. Toronto went on to defeat Milwaukee in the semifinals and then win the NBA Championship for the first time in the team's history.

Other Ventures

Drake's global popularity has attracted the interest of other businesses that believe they could benefit by associating their products and services with the Canadian rapper. In 2015 computing giant Apple approached Drake about assisting with the launch of its music and video streaming service, Apple Music. In a deal that reportedly paid him $19 million, Drake agreed to release his solo music exclusively on Apple Music prior to releasing it to other streaming services and music retailers.

At a victory parade in Toronto, Drake celebrates the Toronto Raptors' 2019 NBA championship with MVP winner Kawhi Leonard. As the team's global ambassador, Drake often talks to the crowd and leads cheers during games.

Drake on Fatherhood

In 2018 Drake announced that he had fathered a son named Adonis with French actress Sophie Brussaux. He discussed fatherhood and his relationship with Brussaux on HBO's talk show *The Shop*, hosted by Maverick Carter and NBA star LeBron James.

> I am a single father learning to communicate with a woman who, you know, we've had our moments, right? And I do want to be able to explain to my son what happened, but I don't have any desire for him to not love his mother. I don't ever want the world to be angry at his mother. We found ourselves in a situation and we are both equally responsible, and now I'm just really excited to be a great father. I have a son. He's a beautiful boy. . . . No matter what happens, I have an unconditional love for the mother of my child, because I want him to love his mother and I have to project that energy.

Quoted in *The Shop*, "Drake Opens Up About His Son Adonis on LeBron's 'THE SHOP' Show," YouTube, October 13, 2018. https://youtu.be/U3l13m_o-rk.

As part of the Apple Music deal, Drake created a radio station dedicated to OVO Sound releases on Beats 1, an online music radio station owned and operated by Apple. The station has become the platform where Drake's newest music is first available. His participation has been credited with making Beats 1 the industry's leading streaming radio service.

Drake has also ventured into the area of food and drink. In 2016 he teamed up with spirits producer Brent Hocking to create a bourbon whiskey called Virginia Black. Drake has promoted the whiskey through his music and tours. For his 2016 Summer Sixteen Tour, for instance, Drake created the Virginia Black VIP Lounge—a high-end ticket package that included samples of the product.

In 2018 he opened a restaurant in downtown Toronto called Pick 6ix. It originally offered menu items from around the world. In

2019 the restaurant became a sports bar called Pick 6ix Sports. The new menu featured pub classics like burgers, pizzas, sandwiches, and fish and chips.

Acting and Producing

Since becoming a music superstar, Drake has taken several breaks from music to return to acting. In 2012 he voiced the character of the wooly mammoth Ethan in *Ice Age: Continental Drift*. He also had a cameo role in *Anchorman 2: The Legend Continues*. He has been the guest host of *Saturday Night Live* twice, appearing in multiple comedy sketches. He has also appeared as himself in various television programs, including *Punk'd*. In 2017 Drake told the *Hollywood Reporter* that he planned to take time off from music to do more acting, but he also said he was going to be extremely selective in the roles he pursued.

Drake is also interested in producing the work of others. He teamed up with NBA great LeBron James to produce the 2017 documentary *The Carter Effect*. The film explores the impact that NBA legend Vince Carter had in Canada when he played for the Toronto Raptors in the late 1990s and early 2000s. Drake is also one of the executive producers of the American teen drama television series *Euphoria*, which is based on an Israeli series of the same name. Like *Degrassi: The Next Generation*, *Euphoria* follows a group of high school students as they navigate contemporary life. Also like *Degrassi*, *Euphoria* explores controversial issues, including sex, drugs, trauma, gender identity, and social media. The series, which stars singer and actress Zendaya, debuted on HBO in June 2019, to mixed reviews that praised the cast's acting but criticized the program's explicit sex scenes.

Private Life

Drake has been romantically linked to many models and celebrities, as well as less-famous women he has encountered on tour and in his everyday life, but he remains unmarried. Early in his career, Drake dated model Catya Washington after she appeared in his "Best I Ever Had" music video. In a 2011 interview, Washington said she and Drake were in love and lived together at one point, but she broke off the relationship when Drake was photographed on dates with exotic dancer Maliah Michel, who starred in the singer's "Find Your Love" music video. Washington says they also broke up because Drake was against her accepting a role in the television series *Bad Girls Club*, while she felt it was an important step forward for her career.

Drake has also been romantically linked with a string of other celebrities, including singer, dancer, and actress Jennifer Lopez; tennis superstar Serena Williams; and a long list of actresses and models. Drake's best-known relationship has been with singer Rihanna. The two superstars dated on and off from 2009 to 2016. Rihanna has had such a big impact on Drake's life that he has mentioned her in all of his studio albums. When he presented Rihanna with the Michael Jackson Video Vanguard Award in 2016,

Drake presents Rihanna with the Michael Jackson Video Vanguard Award in 2016. Drake has been romantically linked with many women, including Rihanna.

he said, "She's someone I've been in love with since I was 22-years-old. She's one of my best friends in the world. All of my adult life I've looked up to her even though she's younger than me."[48]

In a 2018 interview, Drake said that having a family with Rihanna would have been the happy ending to a fairy tale, but it was not to be. Instead, Drake announced in 2018 that a brief relationship with French artist and actress Sophie Brussaux resulted in the conception of a child, Adonis. Drake rarely sees his son, which he poignantly discussed in his 2018 album, *Scorpion*, but he has said that he is determined to change that situation. In March 2019, Drake invited Brussaux to the Paris stop of his Assassination Vacation Tour, and she posted pictures of herself enjoying the concert in the VIP area of the arena. He has also flown her and Adonis on a private jet to be with him on holidays.

Being a parent has proved to be a great inspiration for many artists. If Drake fulfills his goal of spending more time with his son, it is possible that he will likewise mine artistic gold from the stresses, strains, joys, and triumphs of parenthood. It is also possible and even likely that he will continue to write about the twists and turns of his love life. If the day comes when Drake feels he does not have something to say about his life, he plans to retire. "I'm sure I'll stop [making music] one day," he says. "When it starts to feel like I'm making it up. Hopefully I'll catch it before I ever get there, right? But right now it feels like we just started, so I don't plan on stopping anytime soon."[49]

> "[Rihanna is] someone I've been in love with since I was 22-years-old. She's one of my best friends in the world."[48]
>
> —Drake

> "Right now it feels like we just started, so I don't plan on stopping anytime soon."[49]
>
> —Drake

Introduction: Record Setter

1. Quoted in Shakiel Mahjouri, "Drake Talks New Album, Relationship with Nicki Minaj and More," ET Canada, May 3, 2016. https://etcanada.com.

Chapter One: The Family Business

2. Quoted in *Vanderbilt Hustler* (Nashville, TN), "Q & A with Drake," November 28, 2009, p. 20.
3. Quoted in Tatiana Siegel, "Drake's Hotline to Hollywood: Inside an Ambitious Push into Film and TV," *Hollywood Reporter*, November 8, 2017. www.hollywoodreporter.com.
4. Quoted in Jennifer Still, "Drake on 'HYFR' Video Concept: 'I'm a Proud Young Jewish Boy,'" Digital Spy, April 17, 2012. www.digitalspy.com.
5. Quoted in *Vanderbilt Hustler* (Nashville, TN), "Q & A with Drake," p. 22.
6. Quoted in *Vanderbilt Hustler* (Nashville, TN), "Q & A with Drake," p. 22.
7. Quoted *in Degrassi Unscripted*, YouTube, November 5, 2018. https://youtu.be/RHxs3-dLh4k.
8. Quoted in *Degrassi Unscripted*.
9. Quoted in *Drake: Better than Good Enough*, directed by Michael John Warren, aired June 23, 2010, on MTV.
10. Quoted in *Vanderbilt Hustler* (Nashville, TN), "Q & A with Drake," p. 22.
11. Quoted in *Vanderbilt Hustler* (Nashville, TN), "Q & A with Drake," p. 20.
12. Quoted in *Drake: Better than Good Enough*.
13. Quoted in Dalton Higgins, *Far from Over: The Music and Life of Drake, the Unofficial Story*. Toronto: ECW, 2012, p. 13.
14. Quoted in ABC News, "Drake Compared to Will Smith, Linked to Rihanna," YouTube, July 16, 2009. https://youtu.be/3njbUN2RG4s.
15. Quoted in *Vanderbilt Hustler* (Nashville, TN), "Q & A with Drake," p. 21.
16. Quoted in Dailymotion, "Drake on When I Was 17," May 16, 2010. www.dailymotion.com.

Chapter Two: Television Star

17. Quoted in *Degrassi Unscripted*.
18. Quoted in *Degrassi Unscripted*.
19. Quoted in *Degrassi Unscripted*.
20. Quoted in *Degrassi Unscripted*.
21. Quoted in Damien Scott, "Cover Story Uncut: Drake Talks About Romance, Rap, and What's Really Real," Complex, November 6, 2011. www.complex.com.
22. Quoted in Lior Zaltzman, "Drake Sure Knows How to Celebrate His Jewish Momma," *The Schmooze* (blog), *The Forward*, January 29, 2016. https://forward.com.
23. Drake (@Drake), "97% on my final exam. 88% in the course. One of the greatest feelings in my entire life. As of tonight I have graduated high school!," Twitter, October 18, 2018, 5:50 p.m. https://twitter.com.
24. Quoted in Dailymotion, "Drake on When I Was 17."
25. Quoted in Callie Ahlgrim, "The Complete Timeline of Drake's Rise to Stardom, from Starring on 'Degrassi' to His Record-Breaking Reign as a Rapper," Insider, October 23, 2018. www.insider.com.

Chapter Three: Self-Produced Stardom

26. Quoted in Higgins, *Far from Over*, p. 13.
27. Quoted in *Corporate Takeover* (blog), "T.Slack: *The Big Picture*," December 24, 2007. https://corporatetakeover.word press.com.
28. Quoted in Brandon Perkins, "Drake," *URB*, May 2, 2009, p. 41.
29. Guido Stern, "Drake: 'So Far Gone,'" RapReviews.com, February 17, 2009. www.rapreviews.com.
30. Julian Benbow, "Drake, 'So Far Gone,'" *Boston Globe*, March 2, 2009. http://archive.boston.com.
31. Quoted in *Vanderbilt Hustler* (Nashville, TN), "Q & A with Drake," p. 47.

Chapter Four: Chart Topper

32. Bryan Rolli, "'God's Plan' Is Proof That Drake Should Never Release Another Album," *Forbes*, February 15, 2018. www .forbes.com.
33. Quoted in Jonah Weiner, "Weed, Top Chefs and Rick Ross: Drake Ranges Wide on New Album," *Rolling Stone*, July 22, 2011. www.rollingstone.com.

34. Nitsuh Abebe, "Nonstop Pop Machines," *New York*, November 17, 2011. http://nymag.com.
35. Evan Rytlewski, "Drake: *Take Care*," AV Club, November 15, 2011. https://music.avclub.com.
36. Quoted in Nadeska Alexis, "Is Drake the Next Marvin Gaye?," MTV News, September 6, 2013. www.mtv.com.
37. Eric Diep, "Drake Makes His Claim for the Throne with 'Nothing Was the Same,'" *XXL*, September 23, 2013. www.xxlmag.com.
38. Bryant Kitching, "Drake—Nothing Was the Same," Consequence of Sound, September 25, 2013. https://consequence ofsound.net.
39. Quoted in Adelle Platon, "Drake Reveals Kanye West Joint Project Almost Happened & Everything You Need to Know from His Beats 1 Interview with Zane Lowe," *Billboard*, April 29, 2016. www.billboard.com.
40. Elliott Sharp, "Drake's 'VIEWS' Album Breakdown," Red Bull, May 2, 2016. https://www.redbull.com.
41. Andy Gill, "Drake, *Views*—Album Review: 'Rarely Has One Man Moaned Quite So Much,'" *Independent* (London), May 4, 2016. https://web.archive.org.
42. Ryan Dombal, "Drake *Views*," Pitchfork, May 2, 2018. https://web.archive.org.
43. Tommy Monroe, "Drake: *Scorpion*," Quietus, July 4, 2018. https://thequietus.com.
44. Mikael Wood, "Review: On 'Scorpion' Drake Is Tired and Tiring—but as Beautiful an Artist as Ever," *Los Angeles Times*, July 1, 2018. www.latimes.com.
45. Jonny Coleman, "Critic's Notebook: Drake Overplays His Hand on Bloated Double Album 'Scorpion,'" *Hollywood Reporter*, June 29, 2018. www.hollywoodreporter.com.

Chapter Five: Branching Out

46. Quoted in Gregory Babcock, "How the OVO Clothing Label Evolved with Drake's Career," Complex, October 15, 2015. www.complex.com.
47. Quoted Nicholas Hautman, "Drake Responds After Milwaukee Bucks Coach Calls Out His Courtside High Jinks," *Us Weekly*, May 23, 2019. www.usmagazine.com.
48. Quoted in Loulla-Mae Eleftheriou-Smith, "Drake Discusses Relationship with Rihanna at MTV VMAs 2016: 'I've Been in Love with Her Since I Was 22 Years Old,'" *Independent* (London), August 29, 2016. www.independent.co.uk.
49. Quoted in Siegel, "Drake's Hotline to Hollywood."

Important Events in the Life of Drake

1986
Aubrey Drake Graham is born on October 24, 1986, in Toronto, Canada.

1991
Drake begins modeling professionally.

1995
Drake performs "Mustang Sally" onstage with his father at a club in Memphis.

1999
Drake successfully auditions for a part in *Degrassi: The Next Generation*.

2003
Drake takes his *Degrassi* character, Jimmy Brooks, to another level when Jimmy becomes a paraplegic.

2005
Drake is nominated for Best Performance in a TV Series (Comedy or Drama)—Supporting Young Actor by the Young Artist Association.

2006
Drake creates his first mixtape, *Room for Improvement*.

2007
Drake teams up with Trey Songz to create the "Replacement Girl" song and music video.

2008
After hearing Drake's music, Lil Wayne asks the Canadian rapper to join his *Tha Carter III* tour.

2009
Drake releases his third mixtape, *So Far Gone*.

2010
Drake's first studio album, *Thank Me Later*, debuts at number one on the *Billboard* 200.

2011

Take Care, Drake's second studio album, debuts at number one on the *Billboard* 200.

2012

Drake voices the character of the wooly mammoth Ethan in *Ice Age: Continental Drift*.

2013

Nothing Was the Same becomes Drake's third straight studio album to debut at number one on the *Billboard* 200.

2014

Drake hosts *Saturday Night Live* for the first time.

2015

Drake and Future release their collaborative mixtape, *What a Time to Be Alive*.

2016

Drake releases *Views*, his fourth straight album to debut at number one on the *Billboard* 200 and his best-selling album to date.

2017

Sophie Brussaux gives birth to her and Drake's son, Adonis.

2018

Seven singles from Drake's sixth album, *Scorpion*, reach the *Billboard* Top Ten at one time, breaking a record held for more than fifty years by The Beatles.

2019

On August 2, Drake releases his first compilation album, *Care Package*, which debuts at number one on the *Billboard* 200.

Books

Alexis Burling, *Drake: Hip-Hop Superstar*. Minneapolis, MN: Essential Library, 2018.

Barbara Gottfried, *Drake: Rapper and Actor*. New York: Enslow, 2018.

Barbara Gottfried, *Drake: Acting and Rapping to the Top*. New York: Enslow, 2018.

Chris Snellgrove, *Drake*. Broomall, PA: Mason Crest, 2018.

Internet Sources

Callie Ahlgrim, "The Complete Timeline of Drake's Rise to Stardom, from Starring on 'Degrassi' to His Record-Breaking Reign as a Rapper," Insider, October 23, 2018. www.insider.com.

Ben Beaumont-Thomas, "Drake's Progress: The Making of a Modern Superstar," *Guardian* (Manchester), April 6, 2018. www.theguardian.com.

Tatiana Siegel, "Drake's Hotline to Hollywood: Inside an Ambitious Push into Film and TV," *Hollywood Reporter*, November 8, 2017. www.hollywoodreporter.com.

Brianne Tracy, "From Joint Album Teases to Twitter Feuds: A Timeline of Drake and Kanye West's Relationship," *People*, December 17, 2018. https://people.com.

Stereo Williams, "Drake's 2018 Has Been Huge. But Is He the Biggest Rapper Ever?," *Billboard*, July 13, 2018. www.billboard.com.

Note: Boldface page numbers indicate
   illustrations.

Abebe, Nitsuh, 38
acting
   appearing in television as self, 52
   Degrassi: The Next Generation, 5,
      17–21, **19,** 24–25
   desire to return to, 49, 52
   Ice Age: Continental Drift, 5
   Saturday Night Live, 41, 52
Adele, 44
albums
   Nothing Was the Same, 39, 46–47
   Scorpion, 39–40, 43–45
   Soul Movement Vol. 1, 26–27
   Take Care, 37–38, 39
   Thank Me Later, 36, 37
   Views, 39–42, 44, 45
Alexander, Voyce (Clark, Aion), 22
All Things Fresh (record label), 46
Apple Music, 5, 50–51
Assassination Vacation Tour, 40
awards. *See* honors and awards

bar mitzvah, 8–9
Beatles, The, 4
Beats 1 (online music radio station), 51
Benbow, Julian, 32–33
"Best I Ever Had," 33–34
"Best I Ever Had" (music video), 52
Bigger Picture Entertainment, 27
Billboard
   Awards records set by Drake, 44
   Billboard 200 chart, 34, 36, 37–38,
      39–40, 41, 45
   Hot 100 chart, 4, 33–34, 36, 43
   Hot Rap Songs chart, 4, 37
   Hot R&B/Hip-Hop Airplay chart, 4
   Hot R&B/Hip-Hop Songs chart, 33, 34
   Music Awards, 15
   number one debut albums, 39–40
   Rap Songs chart, 34, 36
   Rhythmic chart, 4
   Scorpion debut, 45
   Take Care debut, 37–38
   Top 100 chart, 4
Black Entertainment Television (BET), 29
Brussaux, Sophie, 51, 54
Budenholzer, Mike, 49

Carter, Maverick, 51
Carter Effect, The (documentary film), 52
Champagne Papi, 30
charity, 43
childhood of Drake

acting lessons, 11
   education, 21
   father and law enforcement, 13–14
   friends during, 12–13
   Harry Potter books and, 12
   modeling, 11
   parents' divorce, 5, 8–9
   racial bias and, 12–14
   religion and, 8–9
   songs written by, 13
   time with father, 9–10, 13
Clark, Aion (Voyce Alexander), 22
clothing brand, 47, **48**
Coleman, Jonny, 44–45
Comeback Season (mixtape), 28, 29–30,
   46

Degrassi: The Next Generation (television
   series), 5, 17–21, **19,** 24–25
Diep, Eric, 39
Drake, **6, 10, 19, 31, 34, 38, 43, 50, 53**
   as best-selling recording artist of all
      time, 4
   birth, 8
   as father of Adonis, 51, 54
   love life of, 5–7, 52–54
   on making great music, 41
   motto, 33
   as multitalented artist, 5
   nicknames, 30
   questioning priorities, 37
   wealth of, 5
   See also childhood of Drake; Graham,
      Sandi (mother)
Drizzy Drake, 30

Efron, Zac, 33
El-Khatib, Oliver, 46, 47
entrepreneur, Drake as, 5
   clothing brand, 47, **48**
   television and film productions, 52
   restaurant/sports bar, 51–52
Euphoria (television program), 52

"Fancy," 36–37
film, 5, 52
"Find Your Love," 36
"Find Your Love" (music video), 53
Fiona, Melanie, 22, **22**

Gaye, Marvin, **14,** 39
Gill, Andy, 42
"Girls Need Love," 40
"God's Plan," 36, 43, **43,** 45
"God's Plan" (music video), 43
Graham, Aubrey Drake. *See* Drake

Graham, Dennis (father), 8, 9–10, 13–14
Graham, Larry (uncle), 9
Graham, Sandi (mother), **10**
  on Drake getting part in *Degrassi*, 17
  Drake's public thanks to, 15
  health of, 21, 37
  Jewish faith and, 8–9
  on son's talents and appearance, 11
Grammy Awards
  Best Rap Album, 38
  Best Rap Song, 43, 45
  nominations
    "Fancy," 36–37
    "God's Plan," 45
    "Over," 36
    Scorpion, 45
Grande, Ariana, 40
Green, CeeLo, 22

Harry Potter books, 12
Heartbreak Drake, 30
Hocking, Brent, 51
Hodges, Mabon Lewis "Teenie" (uncle), 9
"Hold On, We're Going Home," 39
Hollywood Reporter, 12, 49, 52
honors and awards
  Juno, **34,** 34–35
  Myspace most-followed musician, 28
  number one songs, 33–34
  Recording Industry Association of America
    records, 4
  records broken by Drake, 4
  See also Billboard; Grammy Awards
Hot R&B/Hip-Hop Airplay chart, 4
Hot R&B/Hip-Hop Songs chart, 33, 34
Hugo, Chad, 16

I Am Music Tour, 31–32
Ice Age: Continental Drift (movie), 5
If You're Reading This It's Too Late (mixtape),
  39–40

Jackson, Michael, 42
James, LeBron, 51, 52
Jay-Z, 42
Jimmy Brooks (fictional character), 17–20
Juno Awards, **34,** 34–35

Kitching, Bryant, 39

Leonard, Kawhi, **50**
Les Misérables (play), 11
Lil Wayne, **31**
  collaborations with Drake, 31–32
  first contact with Drake, 29–31
  "Man of the Year" and, 29–30
  nickname given to Drake, 30

  nickname of, 30
  solo artist record of, surpassed by Drake, 4
  Young Money Entertainment, 35, 36, 46
"Look What You've Done," 38
Lopez, Jennifer, 53
love
  romantic, in Drake's life, 5–7, 52–54
  subject of music, 5, 6–7

"Man of the Year," 29–30
Martin, Aaron, 19–20
Michel, Maliah, 53
"Miss Me," 36
mixtapes
  Comeback Season, 28, 29–30, 46
  If You're Reading This It's Too Late, 39–40
  More Life, 39–40
  Room for Improvement, 24, 26, 27, 46
  So Far Gone, 32–33, 46
  What a Time to Be Alive, 39–40
"Money to Blow," 30
Monroe, Tommy, 44
Montana, French, 40
More Life (mixtape), 39–40
"Motto, The," 33
MTV, 29
Murray, Carmen, 22–23
music, composing and performing
  during childhood, 10, 13
  criticism of, 36, 42, 44–45
  Drake on making great, 41
  early raps, 15
  in family, 9
  music videos
    "Best I Ever Had," 52
    "Find Your Love," 53
    "God's Plan," 43
    "New Joint of the Day," 29
  rapping with Poverty, 15, 20
  raps for *Degrassi*, 20
  Renaissance, 22–24
  Slack as manager, 27–29
  songs on Myspace page, 24, 27
  streaming
    "God's Plan," 36, 43
    records, 4
    Scorpion, 43–44
  studying hip-hop, 15–16
  subjects of songs
    fame, 18
    love, 5, 6–7
  See also albums; mixtapes
Music Awards (*Billboard*), 15, 44, 45
music videos
  "Best I Ever Had," 52
  "Find Your Love," 53
  "God's Plan," 43

"New Joint of the Day," 29
Myspace, 24, 27–28

Nas, 16
National Basketball Association Eastern
    Conference Finals (2019), 49–50
"New Joint of the Day" (music video), 29
Nothing Was the Same (album), 39, 46–47
Notorious B.I.G., the, 16
Nurse, Nick, 49

October's Very Own (OVO), 46–47, **48**
106 & Park (television program), 29
"Over," 36
OVO Clothing, 47, **48**
OVO Fest, 46
OVO Sound, 46

Pick 6ix (restaurant/sports bar), 51–52
Poverty, rapping with, 15, 20
Prince, James "Jas," 30
Promise, 26
Punk'd (television program), 52

racism, 12–14
RapReviews.com, 32
Recording Industry Association of America
    (RIAA), 4, 47
record labels, 26, 35, 36, 46–47
religion, 8–9
Renaissance, **22,** 22–24
"Replacement Girl," 29
Republic Records, 46
"Resistance," 37
Rhythmic chart, 4
Rihanna, **53,** 53–54
Room for Improvement (mixtape), 24, 26, 27,
    46
Rytlewski, Evan, 38

Samuels, Matthew "Boi-1da," 26, 27, **28**
Saturday Night Live (television program), 41,
    52
"Say What's Real," 23
"Say You Will," 23
schwartze, 13
Scorpion (album), 39–40, 43–45
Scott, Travis, 40
Shade 45 (Sirius Satellite Radio), 28
Sharp, Elliott, 42
Shebib, Noah "40," 46, 47
Shop, The (television program), 51
Siegel, Tatiana, 12
"six, the" ("the 6IX"), 40
Slack, Terral "Hollaback" T., 27–29
Slakah the Beatchild, 26–27
Smallz, DJ, 27

"So Far Gone," 33
So Far Gone (mixtape), 32–33, 46
Songz, Trey, 28–29
"Sooner Than Later," 33
Soul Movement Vol. 1 (album), 26–27
Source (hip-hop publication), 28
Sprite, 5
Star Trak movement, 16
Stern, Guido, 32
streaming
    "God's Plan," 36, 43
    records, 4
    Scorpion, 43–44
"Successful," 32, 33, 34
Summer Sixteen Tour, 51
Swift, Taylor, 44

"Tainted" (Slum Village), 22
Take Care (album), 37–38, 39
television
    appearing as self, 52
    Degrassi: The Next Generation, 5, 17–21,
        19, 24–25
    Saturday Night Live, 41, 52
Tennant, Dalton "D10," 22
Thank Me Later (album), 36, 37
Top Rap Albums charts, 38
Toronto hip-hop scene, 26–27, **28**
Toronto Raptors, 5, 40, 48–50, **50,** 52

US Rap Songs chart, 33
US Top R&B/Hip-Hop Albums charts, 38

Views (album, originally *Views from the 6*),
    39–42, 44, 45
Virginia Black whiskey, 51

Walker, Summer, 40
Washington, Catya, 52–53
Weezy, 30
West, Kanye, 23
What a Time to Be Alive (mixtape), 39–40
Wheelchair Jimmy, 30
Williams, Pharrell, 16, **16**
Williams, Serena, 53
Wood, Mikael, 44

XXL (hip-hop publication), 28, 39

YOLO, 33
Young Artist Association acting award
    nomination, 18
Young Money Entertainment, 35, 36, 46
Young People's Theatre (Toronto, Canada), 11

Zendaya, 52
Zimbio (website), 12

PICTURE CREDITS